Horses

Written by Gill Munton

Speed Sounds

Consonants   *Ask children to say the sounds.*

f	l	m	n	r	s	v	z	sh	th	ng
ff	ll	mm	nn	rr	ss	**ve**	zz			**nk**
	le		kn		**se**		se			
					ce		s			

b	c	d	g	h	j	p	qu	t	w	x	y	ch
bb	k	dd	gg		g	pp		tt	**wh**			tch
	ck				ge							

Each box contains one sound but sometimes more than one grapheme.
*Focus graphemes for this story are **circled**.*

Vowels *Ask children to say the sounds in and out of order.*

a	e ea	i	o	u	ay	ee y	igh	ow
at	hen	in	on	up	day	see	high	blow

oo	oo	ar	or oor ore	air	ir	ou	oy
zoo	look	car	for	fair	whirl	shout	boy

Story Green Words

Ask children to read the words first in Fred Talk and then say the word.

horse   born   hay   grass   brush   vet   ill
feed   fast   guard*   Queen   cart   farm   pull

Ask children to say the syllables and then read the whole word.

A|rab   Ex|moor   a|dult   horse|guard*   ex|plore
tran|sport

Ask children to read the root first and then the whole word with the suffix.

breed → breeds   win → winning

*Challenge Words

6

Vocabulary Check

Discuss the meaning (as used in the non-fiction text) after the children have read the word.

	definition
breeds	*different sorts of horses*
Arab horse	*a breed of horse that is clever and strong*
Exmoor	*a wild, open place where few people live*
adult	*a grown-up person or animal*
guard	*to look after someone*

Red Words

Ask children to practise reading the words across the rows, down the columns and in and out of order clearly and quickly.

of	come	there	are
what	mother	water	you
call	who	to	the
was	some	old	want

Breeds of horse

This is an Arab horse.

This is a Welsh Cob.

This horse comes from Exmoor.

There are lots more breeds.

What horses need

When a horse is born, it drinks its mother's milk.

An adult horse needs hay and grass, and water to drink.

If you have a
horse you must:

- feed it
- brush it
- call a vet if it
  is ill.

Snort!

Horses for sport

Horses can run fast.

This horse is winning!

Horses can jump.

This horse is jumping in a show.

Horses on guard

Horseguards are men on horses who guard the Queen.

Horses can help to guard us, too.

Horses for transport

A horse can pull a cart.

This horse is pulling a cart on a farm.

Or you can sit on a horse's back and explore!

Questions to talk about

Ask children to TTYP for each question using 'Fastest finger' (FF) or 'Have a think' (HaT).

p.9   (FF)   Name a breed of horse.

p.10   (FF)   What does an adult horse need to drink?

p.11   (FF)   Name one thing you must do to your horse.

p.14   (FF)   What are horseguards?

p.14   (HaT)   Do horses help to look after people?

p.16   (FF)   Which part of a horse can you sit on?

Questions to read and answer

(Children complete without your help.)

1. When a horse is born, it drinks **water** / **grass** / **its mother's milk**.

2. An adult horse needs **hay** / **meat** / **water** to eat.

3. Horses are good at **skipping** / **singing** / **jumping**.

4. A horse can pull a **farm** / **cart** / **vet**.

5. If your horse is ill you must call a **vet** / **doctor** / **farmer**.